ZOO ANIMALS IN THE WILD

LION

JINNY JOHNSON

ILLUSTRATED BY MICHAEL WOODS

A⁺

Smart Apple Media

Published by Smart Apple Media
2140 Howard Drive West, North Mankato, MN 56003

Designed by Helen James
Edited by Mary-Jane Wilkins
Illustrated by Michael Woods

Photographs by Alamy (James Gritz), Robert E. Barber, Getty Images (Adrian Bailey / Aurora,
Skip Brown, Beverly Joubert / National Geographic, Timothy G. Laman / National Geographic,
Michael K. Nichols, Norbert Rosing / National Geographic, jonathan & angela scott, Manoj Shah,
Cameron Spencer, Justin Sullivan)

Printed in Thailand

Library of Congress Cataloging-in-Publication Data

Johnson, Jinny.
Lion / by Jinny Johnson ; illustrated by Michael Woods.
p. cm. — (Zoo animals in the wild)
Includes index.
ISBN-13: 978-1-58340-899-5
1. Lions—Juvenile literature. I. Woods, Michael, ill. II. Title. III. Series: Johnson, Jinny.
Zoo animals in the wild.

QL737.C23J619 2006
599.757—dc22   2006003059

First Edition

9 8 7 6 5 4 3 2 1

Contents

Lions and lionesses

Lions are among the most magnificent of all creatures. These big, strong cats have a large head, sturdy legs, and a long tail tipped with a tuft of hair. Their fur is a deep golden color.

Male lions are larger and more powerful than females. The male has a mane of hair around his neck and shoulders. This mane becomes fuller and darker in color as the lion grows older. Some old lions have black manes. Female lions are called lionesses.

Lions are some of the most popular animals in zoos. Most large zoos keep lions. There are hundreds of lions living in zoos and animal parks all over the world.

The male lion's thick mane helps protect his head and neck from sharp claws when he fights with other males.

A lion often swishes its tufted tail back and forth to drive away annoying flies.

Teeth, paws, and claws

Big, pointed teeth and powerful, clawed paws are a lion's main weapons for catching food and fighting enemies.

A lion's front teeth are very sharp and can be almost three inches (6 cm) long—about as long as a grown-up's finger.

Most of the time,
a lion keeps its claws
pulled back, out of
the way. But when
a lion wants to
scratch something
or attack prey, it
puts its claws out.

The claws can be pulled
back into special covers
called sheaths. This stops
them from becoming blunt
as the lion walks around.

Every lion has a
slightly different
pattern of spots
above and at the base of
its whiskers.

A lion pride

Lions are the only cats, big or small, that live in groups. A lion family is called a pride. The pride is made up of a group of females, their young, and a few males.

A pride may contain only 4 or 5 lions or as many as 30 or more. Larger prides live in areas where there is plenty of food.

Living in a pride makes it easier to take care of the young. The females in a pride look after the cubs and usually do most of the hunting together.

Most zoos aren't big enough to manage a whole pride of lions, and instead try to keep lions in small groups. Lions aren't happy living by themselves.

The male lions defend the pride against other males. If a stranger comes too close, the male lions attack and drive it away.

The lionesses in a pride often go hunting together.

At home in the wild

Most wild lions live in Africa. The lion is often called the "king of the jungle," but lions usually live in open grasslands, not in forests or jungles.

Male lions guard the pride's territory. They can smell if strangers have been in the area.

Young lions and lionesses are good climbers and like to rest on branches. Full-grown males don't climb much—they are too heavy.

Lions need to live near fresh water so they can have a drink every day.

A few lions live in India, but only in protected areas called reserves.

Every pride of lions has its own special area, called a territory. There must be plenty of prey animals in the territory so the lions have enough to eat. There must be water, too, and hiding places for young cubs. Lions often stay in the same territory for many years.

At home in the zoo

Very few zoos now keep lions in cages.
Lions are big animals and need plenty
of room to move around.

A good zoo makes sure its lions have rocks and other places where they can lie and nap during the day. They need trees or apparatus to climb and somewhere to hide when they don't feel like being stared at.

Wild lions don't eat every day, so most zoos let their lions be hungry one day a week. It's easy for zoo lions to get fat.

Most zoos give lions an indoor den where it is easy for visitors to see the animals up close through the glass.

A lion's day

Lions can seem like lazy animals. They sleep for up to 20 hours a day! The rest of the time, they hunt, defend their territory, and groom each other.

Lions sleep a lot for a good reason. Finding food is difficult and takes a lot of energy. The more a lion moves around, the hungrier it gets. It may catch something to eat only once every two or three days. Resting is a good way to make a meal last longer.

Lions yawn when they are nervous or worried, as well as when they are sleepy.

Zoo lions sleep just as much as lions in the wild. When you go to see them, they'll almost always be taking a nap—unless it's feeding time!

Lions groom each other to remove dirt, blood, and insects from their fur. Grooming is also a good way of showing friendship.

Feeding time

Lions catch and eat other animals. Lions can run fast, but only for short distances. So they sneak up close to their prey before making a high-speed dash and pouncing. Several members of the pride, usually females, hunt together, and the whole pride shares the kill.

A lioness watches her prey carefully before slowly creeping closer.

When a lioness is close enough to her prey, she leaps onto its back to bring it to the ground for the kill.

Large animals, such as wildebeest and zebras, are the favorite prey of lions. But lions also hunt smaller creatures and even steal prey from other hunters. A big lion may eat 100 pounds (45 kg) of meat in one meal—that's like eating 200 big steaks at one sitting! But then the lion won't eat again for a week.

Zoo lions don't have to catch their food. They are given meat and some bones to chew most days. A lion's tongue has a very rough surface, which helps it scrape meat from bones.

Lion babies

A lioness gives birth to between two and five cubs at a time. She keeps them in a safe den away from the rest of the pride for the first few weeks. During this time, the cubs feed only on their mother's milk.

When the cubs are born, they are blind and completely helpless. They weigh around five pounds (2 kg)—about the same as two bags of sugar.

A lion cub can feed from any lioness in the pride, not just its own mother.

The cubs' eyes open when they are between 10 and 15 days old. They grow their first baby teeth at about three weeks of age.

A mother lion moves her cubs to a new hiding place every three or four days. She moves them one by one, carrying them in her mouth.

Zookeepers keep a close eye on mother and cubs when a lioness gives birth in a zoo. She doesn't need to worry about keeping her babies safe.

Growing up

When lion cubs are about six weeks old, they start moving around in their den. Now they are ready to meet the rest of the family. They're nervous at first but soon get used to the other lions.

Lion cubs don't sleep all day like grown-up lions. They like to run and jump.

Cubs feed on their mother's milk for a year or more but start to eat some meat as well at three months of age. Soon they start following their mother when she goes hunting, but they stay out of her way. The cubs grow their adult teeth when they are between 9 and 12 months old.

When a playful cub is too mischievous, its mother may give it a gentle cuff with her paw to say, "that's enough."

Lion cubs learn to hunt their own food by watching their mother —from a safe distance.

Playtime

Lion cubs spend most of their waking hours playing. But play is serious business for young lions. As they play, they are practicing the skills they will need later when hunting and fighting.

Cubs practice their hunting
skills on each other at first.

Young lions in zoos are given plenty of toys to keep them busy and interested—even a roll of cardboard can be lots of fun.

While the older lions snooze, the cubs pounce on their tails and risk a cuff for their boldness. They try to capture insects and chase leaves or anything else that catches their eye. Sometimes the cubs play with the adults, but more often they play with each other.

Play fights are good exercise and help cubs grow stronger.

Keeping in touch

Lions in a pride need to keep in touch, like any family members. Everyone knows that lions roar, but did you know that their roars can be heard as far as five miles (8 km) away?

Lions usually roar at night. They do this to contact other pride members, who might be away looking for food. A lion's roar also tells other lions how big and strong it is.

Lions can tell the roars of other pride members from those of strangers.

This snarling face, with bared teeth, means "keep away from me!"

Lions leave scent messages around their territory by scratching trees or spraying liquid from a gland near their tail. They also do regular checks—sniffing to find out who else has passed by.

Male lions do most of the marking and the patrolling of territories.

Growing older

Lion cubs have a lot to learn. It takes them several years to learn how to catch prey and defend themselves.

Cubs learn to hunt by watching their mother. By the time a cub is a year old, it can kill some prey, and by the age of two, it can hunt alone.

Young lions pay close attention to everything their parents do.

Once a young lion can find its own food, it can survive away from the pride. Many females stay with their mother's pride, but some leave and form new prides. Males always leave the pride in which they were born.

Young male lions usually live alone or with other young males for a few years before finding a new pride to join.

Lion fact file

Here is some more information about lions. Your mom or dad might like to read this, or you could read these pages together.

A lion is a mammal. It belongs to the cat family. Like all cats, a lion is a carnivore, which means it eats meat.

Where lions live

There are lions in parts of east, central, west, and southern Africa, south of the Sahara Desert. They live in savanna areas in countries such as Senegal, Angola, Kenya, and Tanzania. There used to be lions in Asia too, but the only lions left there now are in the protected Gir Forest reserve in India.

Lion numbers

Conservation organizations believe that the number of lions in the wild has gone down by as much as half over the last 20 years. Large areas of their habitat have been destroyed, and lions are still killed by poachers, even though this is against the law. The World Conservation Union (IUCN) lists the African lion as vulnerable. The Asiatic lion is listed as endangered, since there are only about 250 left.

Size

A male lion is between five and a half and eight feet (1.7–2.5 m) long, with a tail measuring about three and a half feet (1 m). Males weigh between 330 and 550 pounds (150–250 kg). Females are smaller—between four and a half and six feet (1.4–1.8 m) long, with a tail slightly shorter than that of a male. Females weigh about 270 pounds (120 kg).

Find out more

To learn more about lions, check out these Web sites.

Big Cat Rescue
http://www.bigcatrescue.org/lion.htm

Smithsonian National Zoological Park
http://nationalzoo.si.edu/animals/greatcats/
lionfacts.cfm

San Diego Zoo
http://www.sandiegozoo.org/animalbytes/
t-lion.html

African Wildlife Foundation
http://www.awf.org/wildlives/148

Words to remember

animal park
A park where lions and other animals can live in the open rather than in cages.

gland
A part of the body that makes a special substance, such as fluid for marking a territory.

mammal
A warm-blooded animal, usually with four legs and some hair on its body. Female mammals feed their babies with milk from their own bodies.

mane
The long hair that grows around a male lion's head and neck.

patrol
To walk around and around a territory, watching out for danger or enemies.

prey
An animal that is hunted and eaten by
another animal.

pride
A group of lions that live in the same territory.
A pride usually has several related females with
their young, as well as one or more male lions.

sheaths
The special covers that protect
a lion's claws when they are
not being used.

territory
The area where an animal spends
most of its time and finds its food.

wildebeest
A large, plant-eating animal that
lives in Africa.

Index